ENEMIES OF PROGRESS

SIMPLE PRINICPLES TO REDEFINE PROGRESS

NATASHA DAVIS

ACKNOWLEDGEMENTS

To my daughter Genesis who has always been my biggest cheerleader, I appreciate having your vote to keep going.

To my parents Joyce Shuman (deceased) and Jerald Ford I could never be here in this place without you.

To my siblings Larry T. Davis, II and Stacy S. Davis (deceased) for we will gather again to laugh and play.

To my spiritual mother Dr. Diane Clark for stretching me and empowering me by just with being in your presence.

Thank you to Tonya Bonner who patiently sat with me once a week until my content was worth editing.

To Billy Ray Davis, Jr. no words can describe the gratitude I have for helping me cross the finish line. You're an amazing friend!

To all my loved ones & friends near and far this is for you.

CONTENTS

INTRODUCTION

This book is not intended to be complicated. It contains simple principles that will allow you to progress in every area in your life.

What does it mean to progress? Progress can be defined as the process of improving or developing over a period of time. It is also considered to be a forward and onward movement toward a particular destination. But defining progress is at best an individual thing. For example, deciding to eat better is a decision that you would make in order to progress in good health. This could even be as simple as adding a cup of water to your daily intake, especially if you previously did not drink water at all.

The decision to progress is also a conscious decision that one makes to do and/or be better. Every year I receive a metabolic panel, which shows how well or poorly I have eaten within a twelve-month period. My cholesterol and sodium levels are measured, and over time, I can see that they have improved or worsened based upon the decisions that I make each day. Therefore, in order for me to progress toward a healthy goal, I must first initiate the process. We are all one igniting decision away from making progress.

If there is a lack of progress in any area of our lives, it can generally be traced back to the decisions that we have made. Just remember that progress begins with a decision and then leads to execution. A great idea will be just that—a great idea in your head—until you decide to act on it. The best vision will be a vision on paper until you decide to execute it.

GOD'S STRATEGY FOR PROGRESS

Jeremiah 29:11 (KJV) states, *"For I know the thoughts I think toward you, saith the LORD, thoughts of peace, and not of evil, to give you an expected end."* This passage expresses God's thoughts towards us

"Be fruitful and multiply" Genesis 1:26 (KJV) are words of expectation for increase, growth, expansion, development, and the furthering and continuation of things that God created. Essentially, God's desire for humanity is that humans will improve, thrive, and achieve great things. The Garden of Eden was created with a manager in mind. Things that grow need management. Wherever there is a garden, there is a strategy for reaping, sowing, tilling, and harvesting. Progress is inevitable in the life of a person who manages productive habits in their lives well. How are you going to manage what you intend to grow? You will need an effective plan of action for what you expect to produce.

We are not in violation of any laws by progressing, but the choice to progress is ours. Going from glory to glory and from faith to faith is an expectation, not a demerit. We have God's earnest permission to move from seed to manifestation and on to multiplication. If you are going to account for your time here on earth, what better way is there to spend your time than to make improvements in your life and community? *"Do not despise these small beginnings, for the Lord rejoices to see the work begin, to see the plumb line in Zerubbabel's hand"* Zechariah 4:10 (KJV). This is a bible passage that is written I believe to encourage us in activities that make our lives better. God rejoices when he sees us our work no matter how small it may seem. Another bible passage says, *"Better is the end of a thing than the beginning thereof."* Ecclesiastes 7:8 (KJV). To start small and increase into something greater is something that we are encouraged to do from a biblical perspective from reading the scriptures above. **Here's a key:** <u>You</u>

<u>can progress by connecting to someone more successful than you in the area you desire to expand, someone else's knowledge and experience can benefit you causing you to grow and evolve to where God is taking you.</u> For you to have something greater, someone will need to expose you to it. God's strategy is to allow growth, but there will be oppositions to your progress. In this book, I will refer to them as enemies.

■ ■ ■

When God gave us life, He already had the end in mind. However, when we begin to get off track and start to move away from the course that would have caused us to arrive at our destination. However, God, through his love, gives us a strategy of navigation by giving us perception of where we are and outlining our steps to get us where we need to be – like a map. Then we are rerouted back to where we need to be at the exact time that we need to be there. For example, administrators in education will map out a course strategy for the program or major that you have selected. And in the event that you do not pass a course, they swoop into action to find recourse for your success. We must also strive to live with a determination to make it to the end of our life course. Our journeys are not perfect paths; therefore, God's strategies must be viewed and accepted as a vital part of our progress. Remember that our daily goal is to progress.

With that in mind, be confident that when things seem to go wrong, the Holy Spirit is operating to make a way out of no way. You will never be stuck when you have developed a strategy of thinking the best about your path in life. With God, all things are possible, and when you keep your options open in Him, every plan will work for your good.

LACK OF STRATEGY

Strategy—do not be intimated by this word. It simply means a plan of action. The plan to lose weight is not a one-size-fits-all concept. Following a basic or generic plan for what you want to accomplish may not be a strategic idea. To be successful, I recommend that you detail your strengths and weaknesses to avoid pitfalls. Writing this book was not an issue for me. One of my gifts is the ability to receive inspirational ideas. However, organizing this book was war! I realized that I was never going to publish a book if I didn't have a strategy to get beyond my weaknesses. Therefore, I enlisted help. The help I received got me over the hump. Having a strategy can include enlisting help.

To illustrate, personal trainers help you get results.

Good personal trainers identify how to help you based on educational experience and good ol' observation. Rather than going to the gym thirty minutes away from work, I go to a location that is fifteen minutes away from work. I noticed that going from the gym to my house cost me time and energy. Yes, that short amount of time wore me out and drained my inspiration. It's as simple as this. Finding another option when you need to—one that works for you—is best to avoid burnout, as we can lose interest in achieving our goals when we feel overwhelmed. I do things simplistically to build the habit or hunger for what I want to accomplish. **Here's a Key:** <u>Make it harder for yourself to quit by making it easier to succeed.</u> I pack my backpack the night before with my gym clothes. I also leave my yoga mat, hand weights, and other accessories in the trunk of my car.

THE ENEMIES

An enemy is a person who is actively opposed to or hostile toward someone or something—a thing that harms or weakens something else. I wrote this book to use as a tool to both expose and identify the enemies of your progress. Many of these enemies worked against me for years, and I was unable to progress in certain areas of my life simply because I wasn't aware of how I was being opposed. Internally and externally, God will not have you ignorant of Satan's devices. I also found that not all of the enemies I had were satanic. You will learn more about this as you read each chapter.

■ ■ ■

THE STARTING POINT

To navigate from one place to another, you must have a starting point. And it is a good practice to identify where you want to go, as well as to determine what may or may not require improvement during the process. An excellent starting point is Philippians 1:6 (NIV) *"Being confident of this, that he who began a good work in you will carry it on to completion until the day of Christ Jesus."* Every good work has a beginning.

■ ■ ■

I can remember that when my daughter was young, she would stand against the wall, and I would mark a spot above her head to measure her height. Every so often, we would check to see how much she had grown by repeating the same steps. Over time, there was a visible trail of markings on the wall from the bottom going upward. As my daughter got older, we were able to see her growth by tracking her progress. It has also been suggested to take before and after pictures as you journey through any process of progression.

While we had our house built, I took pictures of the empty lot. Over time, as the construction went on, I'd show up and marvel at the shape the house was taking. Before long, it would be complete. When the builder invited me in to do a walkthrough, it was no longer a pile of dirt, and the house wasn't actually finished. The drywall, sheetrock, and insulation had been installed. The wiring, plumbing, flooring, and majority of the hardware were visible, but there were still things that needed to be completed. However, I knew that we could make progress by beginning at the starting point.

It was not the appearance of the house that made it home. Instead, it was the process of building, installing, and framing the necessary materials that allowed us to turn a pile of dirt into a place that we were able to call home. If you want to see anything progress or come to pass, you must begin with a starting point.

PART 1

ENEMIES OF PROGRESS

1

PERCEPTION

Whether you are conscious of it or not, other people have their own perceptions of you. When people see you, they have a perception of your dress, your style, and your countenance. But external perceptions do not always line up with internal perceptions.

When we develop perceptions, in short, we interpret or become aware of something. How well do you perceive yourself and your value? Trying to measure up to societally imposed stipulations and standards can be a hindrance to your self-worth. Our experiences in life could either decrease or increase our self-worth. When I became a part of the church, I was so glad to belong to something greater than me. And in the absence of family support, I wanted to belong and to be accepted. So, I took the doctrine and church bylaws to another level! I was extreme in trying to do everything right like show up on time, not miss a Sunday and volunteer for outreach events because I didn't want anything to prevent me from being accepted. Once I realized that I could not win my way into heaven, I embraced grace and the gift of salvation. It took me a long time to cultivate a relationship with Christ because of the wreck I had believed myself to be. Over time, I had to learn that just because something *looks* a certain way, that doesn't mean that it actually *is* that way.

I made the mistake of perceiving myself solely on how I performed. The performance of appearing perfect perception was a great obstacle for me. At one point in my life, my self-image was very poor. When terrible things happened to me, I believed that they happened because I had performed badly. When good things happened to me, again, I thought that they happened because of my performance. From my perspective, it seemed like they couldn't have happened because I was loved, and I did not believe that I would ever be enough to receive God's blessings in my life. I had come from incest, generational curses, and having to deal with being separated from my family.

■ ■ ■

In my mid-twenties, I was due to visit a friend in Atlanta, so I was out getting some last-minutes things into the evening. On my way home, my car started smoking. I noticed that in the car beside me was a man who was looking over at me with concern. I pulled over to see if it was on fire. The man in the car that was next to me pulled behind me. When the man got out of the car, he showed me his military ID and said, "I think you have too much oil." I confirmed that I had put oil in earlier. He then explained that my dad or brother could let a quart out and it should be fine. I thanked him. He said he stopped because he was away all the time and he had a wife and a sister. He hoped that, while he was gone, people would stop to help them since he does good deeds for others.

Just then, a man on a bicycle rode up with a gun and demanded that we both give him our car keys. He took the man's keys first and then threw them over a nearby fence. Then he took my keys and asked me which car was mine and told me to get in on the passenger side. This man drove me someplace I couldn't identify; all I knew was that it was off the main roads. He then parked in an alley. He demanded that I get out of my car and take off all my clothes. Then at gunpoint, he raped me. Afterward, he ran off and left me in my car. I collected myself and went straight home to call the police. Thankfully, the police were already looking for me. The military man had called the police and reported what had happened. I had been abducted, robbed, and raped at gunpoint. Unfortunately, they were ultimately unable to find the guy who committed this crime against me.

My understanding of the world was based on my experiences and not on the word of God. My understanding didn't come from any positive conversations I was having with others. And with my actions being a direct result of what I had gone through and not solely a result of me becoming a product of my environment, there was still a chance for me to move beyond performance and begin to see myself how God sees me.

■ ■ ■

In the years since that traumatic episode, I have learned that the most important dialogue was internal. Self-dialogue is the thoughts and conversations you have inside your head that describe how you truly see yourself. For example, I would say negative things in my thoughts like, "you never do what you say you are going to do. You never finish anything. You are not good enough to have what you want." This would bring my excitement down discouraging me to follow through on the plan. Thoughts like, "you can't do it it's too hard, no one is going to read your book, no one is going to listen to you." I have a bright idea to start a fitness plan then my internal voice would say, "you're lazy and aint gonna do nothing!"

To change this dialogue from negative to positive, I cultivated a habit to confront negative thoughts not allowing them to rule my internal voice. When I would have a negative thought speaking about my actions of lack of actions I begin reciting Philippians 4:13 (KJV) *"I can do all things through Christ that give me strength."* I also examined if the thoughts are how I think or feel about me or if they came from someone else like a family member or friend. I can remember having an argument with one of my girlfriends that said I let her down. Her words became an internal conversation in my head that all I do is let people down. After thinking about it I had recalled being there for her so many times so if I missed one time so what! I began affirming I was a reliable friend in my own voice and refused to think otherwise. Be careful that you do not have someone else's negative voice trapped in your head. **Here's a key:** <u>Take a stand say what God says about you often so that you will cultivate a positive internal voice.</u> Positive internal dialogue will help you progress in how you see yourself.

PHYSICAL IMAGE

This image is not just the dimensions of your height or the color of your hair and eyes. It's more than what size shoes and clothes you wear. It's not about being an endomorph (a pear shape), a mesomorph (an hourglass shape), or an ectomorph (a rectangular shape). The origin and history of languages can improve our understanding of the words we use and give a precise meaning to them. With that in mind, the word *Morph* originates in the Greek language and it means "shape;" it gives a description to the physical image. The word *Figura* is the Latin root word for shape means "form." Mankind was created in God's image and made in his likeness. I personally believe we are morphed, which can also mean that we may make gradual steps toward change. As we age, we are subtly changing day by day. No matter how much time and money we spend on our appearance, we will all, at some point, age.

Men and women both go through these changes in life in some form or another. Typically, when men age, they are challenged by their body image. For example, they may struggle with their hair turning gray or with losing hair. Instead of making safe, smart decisions about their future, they may become more adventurous, making purchases like sports cars, motorcycles, and trendy clothing.

■ ■ ■

The reality of change will eventually show, though, no matter the person's gender. Women will go through changes in life, as well. We will pass through our childbearing years whether we have children or not. By design, we go from one form to another throughout the course of life. I remember an episode from *The Cosby Show* when Rudy was having the return-to-school blues because she had not transformed physically over the summer. All of her friends were wearing bras except her. After having a hard time accepting the truth that her body had not changed the way she thought it would. She took the advice of her mom, who told her, "You get what you get when you get it and not before then." If we are going to progress, we must plunge into the depth of who we are and not be disturbed or distracted by the constantly changing forms of our bodies or the bodies of others.

MENTAL IMAGE

One of the side effects of being raped is mental impairment after the attack. Post-Traumatic Stress Disorder (PTSD) impacts people in a variety of ways, depending upon the background of the individual and how the trauma took place. It is important to have a healthy mental image of yourself. Progressing means that you are not boxed into what has happened to you. Life is hard enough, especially when you grow up under peer pressure. We experience challenges as adults, as we take care of ourselves, have careers, and start our own families. **Here's a key**: <u>Having the confidence to cope with life as it happens will empower you.</u>

■ ■ ■

Blaming yourself for things you could not control is not healthy. The way you think is valuable to your quality of life. As a teen, I blamed myself for my family's issues. My siblings and I spent time in foster care. I found letters that revealed that my sister was sexually active with the man who had been introduced to me as my dad. In these letters, she wrote that she loved him and was pregnant. I was eleven years old, she was thirteen, and my brother was fifteen years old. I thought that this was not right, but at eleven years old I could not process it, so I took the letters to my mom. Over the next few days, she got around to reading them, and life shifted for the worse. Because of the disruptions in the house over the news that my mom had received, a neighbor got involved by calling the Department of

Children and Family Services. We were all taken from the house and separated. I thought to myself, if I had kept the letters to myself, this would not have happened. Blaming myself for my parents' troubles made me feel unwanted. My mom had reunited with my dad after years of being out of touch. Before they reunited, no one really told me who my father was. So, when I was introduced to him at nine years old, I had a lot of questions. Overall, I was glad my family was finally getting stable. I was excited to be in a house with a yard in a good neighborhood and no longer living in an apartment or from this place to that place. The family split happened when I got used to sleeping in my own bed beginning to adjust to a new way of living. After being away from my family I felt I was the cause of so much pain I attempted suicide later at the age of fourteen. Clearly, I did not succeed; however, this mindset of blame came with me into my early adulthood. Every time something didn't work, I suffered from depression. I believed it was my fault. You would be surprised the progress you can make in your life and relationships with the right mindset and mental image. I began to advance in life once I got my head together believing in myself. Thus, being able to cope with adversity in a healthy manner rather than having an emotional collapse.

FINANCIAL IMAGE

Cultures can create financial images. Some people may think that having millions of dollars will give you a sense of security. The life of John Paul Getty will teach you differently. Mr. Getty was rich, yet he felt less secure with each dime he made. He lived in solitude and died alone, thinking that all people wanted from him was his money. He created a negative financial image for himself, which he based on his own perception. He had many possessions. He became a swindler and learned various ways to hide his money in foreign accounts. How you see yourself—with or without money—speaks to the level of your soul's wealth and prosperity. Living in the slums or ghettos doesn't make *you* ghetto—it's the image painted in your mind from the culture you were morphed (shaped) in. I have seen devout, respectable people without a dime behave in a dignified manner. I have also seen these people be just as well read as a person with money.

Dr. Maya Angelou said it well: "I can be changed by what happens to me. But I refuse to be reduced by it." Making more or less money will only affect you negatively if you believe the image formed in the process. The man who earns a lot of money and likes pretty women will flaunt his money to attract a pretty woman because he lacks a positive self-image. When she discovers he is u-g-l-y on the inside, she won't stay. **Here's a key:** <u>Having self-confidence—with or without money—will make you that much more attractive to others.</u> Whether I buy an outfit from Goodwill, Target, Ann Taylor, or Nordstrom's doesn't make a difference. God's favor makes me rich. *"The blessings of the Lord make one rich and add no sorrow,"* Prov. 10:22 (KJV),

INTELLECTUAL IMAGE

In 1998, I met a guy who was really smart. His name was William. I was so impressed with how well spoken and knowledgeable he was. In my eyes, he sparkled like brand-new jewelry. Let me remind you—I did not get a high school diploma until I was twenty-five years old. Up until that point, I was not studious. In fact, I was struggling to read my Bible and follow the lessons taught in church. I became a good listener and note taker, even though I wasn't spelling half the words correctly.

I loved that William was a reader. I was smitten. He was a history major, so he knew lots of facts—facts about the Bible, geography, archeology, and science. He was a walking encyclopedia. I did not grow up with people telling me I was smart, but I knew clearly what it meant to not be smart. It meant people would take advantage of you if you couldn't count. It meant you could be easily manipulated and used. I learned some street smarts from being on the street as a runaway. I saw drug deals, prostitution, domestic violence, and the like. You name it—I saw it. I was clear on how to adjust to different environments because I knew that if I didn't, it could cost me my life. But William was different—very different. We met at the church. His family was very involved there, so I began to see him all the time. Each time I saw him, he had some information or facts to give me. I was becoming his student. As much as he wanted to talk, I listened. Eventually, I shared with him that I had dropped out of junior high and did not have a diploma. Without blinking an eye, he said, "You are intelligent enough to have one if you wanted it."

We hung out all the time, but because I was insecure about not having a high school diploma at the age of twenty-five, I saw myself as less than him. I was a grasshopper in my own eyes just like the children of Israel saw themselves compared to the giants in a land that had been promised to them. There I was, thinking, I don't have anything. Why does he want to hang out with me? Because I had a warped self-perception from the abuse I had endured, I thought he must have a hidden agenda. The only agenda he had was to convince me that I was worth more than I believed.

In like manner, know that people are not always drawn to you because of how you look or what you know. Take heart from my story that God can cause people to invest in you because you have potential and are worth the investment. To this point, as God was choosing another king for Israel here is what he shared *"But the Lord said to Samuel, "Do not look on his appearance or on the height of his stature, because I have rejected him. For the Lord sees not as man sees: man looks on the outward appearance, but the Lord looks on the heart," 1 Sam. 16:7 (KJV).*

William said that he knew people who were educated and not as real as I was (meaning genuine). He was able to be real with me about his struggles and issues. His colleagues and friends were more interested in his status, rather than who he was as a person. I stayed real with him. That was twenty-one years ago, and I'm still the same person today. I learned later that I was structured, determined, reliable, and trustworthy. William went on to be a college professor. He was a teacher at heart and was drawn to me by my thirst to learn. Why did I share this story with you? To let you know that having an education does not make you who you are; it can only encourage you to use information.

Here's a key: <u>If you are going to progress in life, you must see yourself the way God sees you.</u> If you are going to progress in life, you must renew your mind. Romans 12:1 (ESV) says, *"But be transformed by the renewal of your mind, that by testing you may discern what is the will of God, what is good and acceptable and perfect."*

If you are going to progress in life, you must cast down thoughts and images of yourself that do not reflect the love of Christ for you. Proverbs 23:7 (KJV) says, *"As a man thinks in his heart, so is he."* You will be whatever you think about yourself. Cast down every imagination—by this, I mean any image that was placed in your mind by something you perceived. Calling yourself dumb, stupid, or an idiot does not improve your self-perception; instead, it bruises it. Using affirming statements daily to transform how you see yourself and feel about yourself is vital.

■ ■ ■

Create a personal affirmation, or use one that you have heard someone else say. I look in the mirror and say, "I can do it with the help of the Lord," which comes from Philippians 4:13 (KJV), *"I can do all things through Christ which gives me strength."* When I fall short of the courage I need to do great things I repeat this scripture as affirmation and it makes a big difference in how I think.

■ ■ ■

SELF-IMAGE

An identity crisis is a period of uncertainty or confusion in which a person becomes insecure due to a significant change, which often includes a role change, in his or her life. At some, we all will experience this. For example, let's say that you were married but then go through a divorce. In this instance, a change in your name and responsibilities may make you feel unsure of yourself. If you have been diagnosed with an illness that causes your strength to no longer be what it used to be, you may begin to question yourself. Ironically, a great epiphany could happen in a crisis, and it could allow you to discover who you are.

Knowing who you are is having a revelation of who you are. I discovered certain truths about myself that showed me what my abilities were. The more certain I was of my abilities, the more confident I was. In *Spirit-Controlled Temperament*, Tim LaHaye writes that:

"Maestro Melancholy is often referred to as the "black" or "dark" temperament. Actually, he is the richest of all of the temperaments, for he is an analytical, self-sacrificing, gifted, perfectionist type with a very sensitive, emotional nature."

The above quote is a brief description of my character traits. Discovering Tim LaHaye's research on my temperament gave me a boost of confidence to accept that I would do great things. When you are convinced of who you are—when there is no question of who you are—your confidence will soar. Embracing your strengths allows you to be calm so that when someone else brings your weaknesses to your attention, you won't be thrown off guard.

■ ■ ■

KNOWING WHO YOU ARE

Knowing who you are will help you know who you click with and who you clack with. My temperament is melancholy; I am an introvert, analytical, a perfectionist, quiet, creative, and a critic. Learning who I am made me embrace myself. Just live with who you are, and as the Lord moves in your heart to change and transform you, that is when change happens. Trying to be someone you are not will only make you miserable. You will not be pulled into something that you are not. You will set people straight when they try to force you to be something or someone you are not. My temperament is melancholy. Yes, I am an introvert, which means I enjoy people, but I enjoy being alone more. I feel suffocated when I am with people more often than I am alone. Because I know this about myself, I feel empowered. I have progressed in developing my interpersonal skills because I have learned who I am. As a melancholy person, I admire the characteristics of others, I am able to maintain inner peace because I am convinced that I have the best temperament of them all. Biased? Absolutely! Why be down about who you are? Besides, all temperaments bring things with them into the world that will cause them to progress in life.

My temperament causes me to prolong things because I want to be perfect. This was a challenge for me until I discovered my identity in Christ. I am the righteousness of God in Christ Jesus and no longer perform to be good. I attribute this liberation to 2 Corinthians 5:21(WE) "Christ did no wrong thing. But for our sake God put the blame for our wrong ways on Christ. So now God sees us as good, because we are in Christ." Therefore, I don't have to be perfect. I have instead replaced perfectionism with excellence. The Bible speaks about having an excellent spirit. I can have an excellent spirit without the pressure of trying to be something unachievable. Our temperaments have a nature that will offer us a challenge—everyone is included. **Here's a key:** <u>If you are going to progress, knowing the habits of your nature is important</u>. If your chosen career or business requires you to be people oriented, but your temperament is introverted, then learning to control your natural inclination is necessary to build the customers and clients that you need to have a successful business. In your quest to discover your temperament, you must know that you will see yourself as the friend and others as the villains. Be open to the enemies within to get a true picture of your behaviors. Then when it comes to discovering the temperaments of others realize that you can learn which temperaments you work with best.

GOT CONFIDENCE?

Confidence can come from knowing you are right. Have you ever been in a discussion and you were confident in what you were saying, no matter who you were saying it to, because you just *knew* that you were right? A confident heart is to be at the center of who we are. My favorite color is black. Some people think black is plain and basic. Once I worked part time in an upper-class retail store. A lady working as a hostess was looking for a black shirt. As she approached me, she said,

"I am looking for a basic black shirt." I smiled at her and very confidently said to her, "black is anything but basic! Black is classy, black is sexy, black is powerful, black is bold—black is always the right color for any occasion." Because I ran off this list of what black is, the lady changed her physical posture and looked thrilled that I had given her my observation of black. She then bought two blouses for work. I knew then that I had made a believer of this customer—all because I was confident about my favorite color. It wasn't rehearsed; it was free-flowing and spontaneous. I am not much an of salesman, but I stand by what I am confident about.

Therefore, a confident attitude can convince you to buy a blouse, a television, a new car, or even go out on date. Confidence can get in a great door of opportunity, employers can be convinced you are the right person for the job if you speak in confidence. Time with a person speaking in a persuasive tone can be very convincing. We see this skill in actors who play roles that bring the character to life. Specifically, let's look at Denzel Washington's role in the movie *Training Day*. He played a ruthless drug dealing cop, it was so convincing he won an Oscar for his performance. What really won the Oscar and made the movie so believable was confidence. On the contrary, the negative words in the back of your mind wants to convince you that you cannot progress. Likewise, this is Satan's plot against you. He wants to convince you of the same. He is confident that his methods will work against you for you to fail. In *A Confident Heart*, Renee Swope writes, "We have an enemy who wants to convince us that he is the only one who can change things. He wants us to doubt God's sovereignty and question His ability to care for us." Even Satan has confidence. He believes he can convince you to be against God and the abilities given to you to progress in life. This simply isn't true! Jesus says, *"The thief cometh not, but to steal, and kill, and to destroy: But I am come that they might have life and that they might have it more abundantly,"* John 10:10 (KJV). If you are going to progress you must be confident in that you are going to live an abundant life.

No matter what, confidence can be part of your temperament. I recall a conversation I had with a friend. I was certain that my facts were right. I was quoting a line in a movie scene. My friend knew the scene so well. He said, "You're loud and wrong!" Then he preceded to recite the quote verbatim. Strong debates, rebuttals, responses, replies—these all come from having confidence. Jesus was in a place of weakness, but he was confident as he told the devil, *"Man shall not live by bread alone but by every word that proceeds out of the mouth of God."* Matthew 4:4 (KJV) He had fasted forty days and was hungry, yet his confidence in the truth was strong. **Here's a key:** <u>A weapon against the enemy of your progress is a confident heart!</u>

■ ■ ■

It took confidence for me to write this book. This is my first book to be published. To not publish this book would mean that I did not believe in my abilities. Believing in my abilities does not make me perfect. It only allows me an opportunity to show you that confidence can empower you, which will allow you to progress. I wasn't always confident. Could it possibly be that I have a gift to write and that I believed that where I came from, who my parents are, and my level of education and social class all held me back? Absolutely!

■ ■ ■

It is so important to know your identity, as therein is your purpose. More than my abilities, I believe in God's purpose for me. I have come to trust that if God has a purpose for us, then we have abilities that allow us to fulfill our purpose. You may have to cultivate your potential to fulfill a purpose. You were made in the image and likeness of God above all. What I mean by that is even though we are born into families, our family culture can taint the pure image placed in you by God. We learn mostly everything from those who fed us, changed our diapers, and clothed us. Repeating negative things that we have heard will not reflect who we were created to be. We can inherit positive things like being a great cook or the best housekeeper on the planet yet lack purpose.

To the point, positive things can be on the inside of us being reminded that we resemble respected people in our families can give us a boost of confidence we need to do great things. Hearing someone say, you sing like your grandmother, or you are athletic like your father not only makes you smile but it implies you can do something great too and that you have purpose. To give his mentee Timothy a boost of confidence the Apostle Paul shared how Timothy's faith comes from generations before him and it was visible in his life as well. *"I am reminded of your sincere faith, which first lived in your grandmother Lois and in your mother Eunice and, I am persuaded, now lives in you also," 2 Timothy 1:15 (KJV).*

By Him, you are born, and by Him, you inherent the genealogy to produce and manifest great things. Many doctors hail from generations of doctors. The same holds true with any profession. Likewise, in faith, you can inherit and assume the identity of faith from your family. If there were none, then your spiritual parents assume this role. By spiritual parents I mean the people that nurtured your faith, spiritual practices, or influenced your growth maybe they called or identified by another name in your cultural influence but they took personal and special interest in your well-being as the Apostle Paul did for young Timothy.

■ ■ ■

I don't hail from a lineage of authors, yet I can see where entrepreneurship has been in my family for generations. Now that I have published a book, others in my family may gain the confidence to do so, as I had the confidence to be the first.

■ ■ ■

Genetics play an important role in our identity, and the environment that we grow up in shapes us; however, we don't have to remain beholden to our genetics and environment. I had a rough upbringing. I'm confident that my mother did the best she could, yet we faced many challenges as a family. Eventually, we were torn apart when I was young. As an adult, I can look over my life and see what I inherited from my mother. She recently passed away, but I often reflect and admire many traits about her. She was a great cook, and she kept her home tidy, so likewise I exercise the same practices. Progress is both inheritance and the process of cultivation.

2

COLD FEET

The definition of "cold feet" is apprehension or doubt strong enough to prevent a planned course of action. Progress requires courage. Fear is a stagnating enemy. Fear is a tactic. Fear is also a strategy to interfere with your progress. Without a doubt you must intimidate your rival refusing to be inferior. A rival is someone who is competing to be superior to you. You are an opponent, a contender. Your enemy's role is to oppose you. I have experienced the most fear when treading on new ground. Whenever I take on something big, my heart needs strength from the Father.

The prophet Elijah had a big mission: to destroy the prophets of Baal and Asherah, about eight hundred fifty bad guys. This made Jezebel furious, so she sent a message to Elijah that she would do the same to him. Fear struck Elijah, and he ran. He prayed that God would let him die.

■ ■ ■

Bold assignments require you to guard your heart. There are two personal revelations I have first is that when preachers kneel to pray, they acknowledge and take on a shield that guards them against the attacks of the enemy. Secondly, I've seen football players go to the field and kneel to pray before the game starts. This a guard against fear. Shield your heart during your assignment. Your heart can be open during the assignment, but fear can creep in because of the size of your assignment. The breastplate of righteousness is a tool against fear. Moreover, the Bible refers to it as armor. Ephesians 6:11-14 (NIV) says:

"Put on the full armor of God, so that you can take your stand against the devil's schemes. For our struggle is not against flesh and blood, but against the authorities, the powers of this dark world and against the spiritual forces of evil in the heavenly realms. Therefore put on the full armor of God, so that when the day of evil comes, you will be able to stand your ground, and after

you have done everything, to stand. Stand firm then, with the belt of truth buckled around your waist, with the breastplate of righteousness in place, and with your feet fitted with the readiness that comes from the gospel of peace. In addition to all this, take up the shield of faith, with which you can extinguish all the flaming arrows of the evil one. Take the helmet of salvation and the sword of the Spirit, which is the word of God."

All apprehension is removed knowing that my success is not solely based on how I perform. I am also protected against believing I will fail present, past or future.

THE PAST

Feeling condemned by your past decisions will not make you feel worthy to have the promises of God articulated throughout the bible. Specifically, *"If we confess our sins, He is faithful and just and will forgive us our sins and purify us from all unrighteousness,"* *1 John 1:9 (KJV).* Feeling disapproved or strongly criticized will hinder your pursuit of the future. These feelings could overwhelm us. Knowing the promises of God encourages us that we are acceptable. Nothing in our past can stop God's forgiveness and loves towards us. All we have to do is accept that his words are true. Another promise is what God thinks about us and our future, *"I know the plans I have for you, declares the Lord, plans to prosper you and not harm you, plans to give you hope and a future,"* Jeremiah 29:11 (KJV).

When you see yourself in a small way, you will perceive in a small way. You will see things from a small angle. This insignificant perception is in your own eyes. As the spies went to look at the land that God had given them, all but two men brought back a report based on their perception of being incapable to move into the land because giants dwelled there. Joshua and Caleb were not intimidated by what they saw. The others with them was minimized by perception comparing themselves to grasshoppers against not only the size of the fruit but the size of people dwelling there. This story recorded in the bible can be found in Numbers chapter 13.

There is a problem when God has given you something that you feel like you are too small to possess it. Adam said to God, *"I was afraid because I was naked; so, I hid,"* Genesis 3:10 (NIV). Adam was not created by God with this perception of himself. Something happened to shape his perception into a negative view. Feeling small and ashamed is not what God intended for his children to perceive. Deception is behind a small perception. After Eve was deceived, she and Adam took on a more insignificant perception of themselves no longer were they confident but rather they were timid and ashamed.

■ ■ ■

Make sure you know that you are not in competition with your past. There was a reason that God advised Lot not to turn back to Gomorrah, as doing so would cause him to turn into a pillar of salt. When you are looking back, you identify with who you were and what you felt in the past. You could be pulled back into the guilt and pride and live in past, although none of what you see as you glance back is actually real.

Likewise, the children of Israel complained about the food they were eating. They compared it to the food that prisoners would eat. The food you eat as a free person or in your progressed life will always be better than what you experienced when you were in chains.

■ ■ ■

You can grow accustomed to what you have been exposed to—for instance, Venus and Serena Williams were exposed to tennis in their youth. Likewise, Tiger

Woods played golf when he was a child. They may not have been exposed to fame and riches. If they were not, this was cultivated in their lives at some point. It takes courage to cultivate something new in your life. Oprah Winfrey has shared a trying part of her life. She grew up poor, and once she became rich and famous, she was challenged to say no to all the relatives and friends pursuing her for money. Oprah explained that it took courage to live a progressive and successful life. Progressing in life may gain you some attention, perhaps. Success—no matter how great or small—requires courage. Standing up to others and facing the conflicts you have to navigate in relationships, money, and decisions all require courage.

This is especially true if your decisions are not popular. I have a great appreciation for my daughter Genesis. As a teen, she often asks questions for guidance and understanding. One day, she asked, "What do you do when you have a standard and the people around you don't meet that standard?"

"Prepare to walk alone," I replied. As a teen facing the pressures of sex, drugs, driving without a license, and other activities that complicate your life, you will need the courage to stand up for yourself. Your peers may see you as lame and call you a square and other names associated with being responsible, but it is important to be courageous as you stand up for the decisions you make. I have had to say no to my abusers, and I had to stand up for myself. Circumstances and bad outcomes were my teachers. I learned to stand up for myself when I was being penalized for being a female. At the time, I was a child with no advocate to stand up for me. Even as a young adult, to get out of trouble, I had to speak up for myself. Since I made my transition into adulthood by lying on my application to get an apartment, I was not exposed to what I actually needed to do to maintain a household. In my late teens years to avoid being in a foster home I had been living with a man twice my age, and I was not taught to balancing a checkbook. I wrote checks that bounced. For those of you who have not been exposed to what writing a bad check means: before debit cards, you could write a postdated check. If the check did not clear, it was returned unpaid to the company. Since I had not yet learned money management by this point, I was raking up debt in checks that did not clear my account because I assumed responsibility without exposure. This is against the law! I was arrested for this and spent the night in jail. The next day in court, I was in handcuffs and orange scrubs. This predicament gave me the courage to speak out to explain why I was in this situation. The judge was about to sentence me to thirty days in jail until I pleaded that I would pay the money back, but if I was going to jail, I'd lose my job. I was not a Christian yet, so hallelujah was not in my spirit, but I was so relieved when the judge said that I did not have to go back to jail! Yes, a twenty-four-hour jail experience gave me the courage to never be in that situation again. I struggled to learn money management at nineteen years old as well as over the next couple of years, but that was the introduction to being self-sufficient and learning what it meant to be responsible for myself. I realized I needed to have the courage to change and grow.

Another time I found courage was when I was hospitalized for a urinary tract infection and dehydration. I passed out suddenly and woke up with the worst back pain I'd ever had in my life. The infection occurs in the bladder or kidney areas of the body Again, I lacked exposure to eating healthy and drinking water, along with what *not* doing these things would do to your body. There I was, barely awake and in immense pain as I was positioned on my side when the doctor came in and asked, "How do you feel?" Before he could tell me not to move, I began to do so, and it felt like I had pins sticking me in every direction. He explained that I was dehydrated and that I had a catheter inserted so that I could go to the bathroom. He explained I that I also was receiving (IV) Intravenous therapy, a method by which fluids go directly into the vein. He proceeded to tell me that I was on antibiotics to treat the urinary tract infection (UTI) and would not be eating for the next two days. I was only allowed to have clear liquids—water, Jell-O, and popsicles.

I wondered how this could have happened, how did I get to such a state? The nurse came in after the doctor left to explain that I needed to finish the pitcher of water on the tray beside the bed. As she was talking, I was reflecting on how I hated water, and then she touched my lower side of my back. I almost jumped out of the bed! Oh, my goodness! It was excruciating! After one touch, I was vomiting, and my head was pounding. I was so weak that I slept until the next day. I was only twenty-one years old, and I felt like I had been run over by a Mack Truck, but somewhere in the middle of it all, I found the courage to do something I hated. Because I wanted to never feel this way again, I pinched my nose and drank water until I was able to use the bathroom on my own. I was told to drink it until my urine was clear each day after I was released.

At discharge, an older nurse said, "Until you are able to tolerate the taste of water, use one quarter cup of cranberry juice or apple juice to eight ounces of water." I eventually began drinking water without anything to mask the taste. This progress caused me to never experience bladder or kidney issues again. When people think of courage, they usually think of gigantic things, but honestly, there is no small courage or big courage—no big faith or small faith. It takes courage to drink water when you hate it or to learn to manage your checking account when you are intimidated and have no idea what you are doing. No matter what, courage will see you through. If you are going to progress you will need courage. **Here's a key:** <u>The source to having courage is to find what motivates you.</u> In the stories I shared motivation and courage can be found in what you don't want to happen as much as the good things you desire to happen.

3
RUNNING WILD

There's nothing scarier than being somewhere and not knowing where you are. A child separated in the grocery store from a parent will panic because she feels lost. When you are in the middle of nowhere in desperate need of direction, it becomes so valuable when you finally receive it. When you know where you're going, you have confidence and peace. There are times in our lives when we are sure we don't know where we are going, yet we still drive through the neighborhood or a highway, hoping to see a familiar landmark

When we have direction—which is another word for management and administration—we have a way of doing things. Direction is not limited to instructions to a physical destination; it is also leadership and guidance. I value direction at this point in my life like never before. When you are facing critical situations in your life, such as foreclosure, bankruptcy, or divorce, it is vital to know which direction to go in to get help or to find a path that will lead to safety. These are examples of how leadership is useful. Your path determines your progress.

■ ■ ■

I have always had success asking others for guidance when I was limited in experience and information. I experienced limited success when exercising on my own; however, asking a more experienced person for guidance allowed me to achieve my fitness goals and do so more efficiently. I see people at the gym all the time running wild. They slam down the weights as they finish and make loud grunts. Often people on the machines seem aloof and emotionally disconnected from the activities they are engaging in. Why do anything if it's not going to place you where you want to be? Remember that progress is a conscious decision that one makes to be better. Deciding to do nothing by default is also a decision.

■ ■ ■

Going to various places with no clue what you are doing or where you are going is what I call running wild—and running wild without a route, no less. In this case, you move aimlessly on your own, unlike a herd of animals heading in the same direction. A herd of wild animals follows a flow. They run in the same direction. Even nature has a process for how things move along. Rivers have a flow, and everything in the river follows a flow of how things move along. Nature has a process of development. A life with no direction is a life not following a vision. The Bible says it like this: "*Where there is no vision [no revelation of God and His word], the people are unrestrained,*" *Proverbs 29:18b (AMP)*. **Here's a key:** <u>If you are going to progress, you will need direction.</u> Now is a good time to ask yourself, are you running wild in your business ideas, finances, family, education, or relationships? Are the critical situations in your life lacking a destination and an idea of how to get there? "*Wisdom and money can get you almost anything, but only wisdom can save your life,*" *Ecclesiastes 7:12 (NLT)*.

■ ■ ■

The movie *Waiting to Exhale* has a character named Robin. She got into a quick relationship with a man she had only known for four days. In that time, her wallet came up missing. Robin found out that her love interest was a crackhead. She was clueless—so are many of us when it comes to following our emotions. There is nothing more terrible than being in a crisis and needing information or help and not having a source available to help. We have to begin to view a lack of knowledge as a crisis, rather than believing that what you don't know can't hurt you. *"My people are destroyed from a lack of knowledge," Hosea 4:7 (KJV).*

■ ■ ■

UTTER FOOLISHNESS

Foolishness is a lack of good sense. Before you question why this section is in this book or you decide not to read it altogether, let me share with you the value of this chapter. I wrote a poem titled "Don't Be Stupid" when I was being stupid. You are being strung along, and your conscience is telling you that something isn't right. Yep, it's screaming at you to be smarter. Business and relationships require wisdom and sound judgment. Otherwise, you can lose your life savings or waste valuable time being senseless. This is counterproductive, and it is an enemy to your progress. **Here's a key:** <u>Apply intentional effort where you need and desire progress.</u>

■ ■ ■

"Lord, I don't want to be without your guidance. Don't take your Holy Spirit from me." I often pray this prayer when seeking guidance and direction. We can be so excited for good news and good tidings that we become gullible. Excitement does not have to equate to silliness. While we do not have to live a life of being suspicious of everything or everyone, we must live a life of good judgment if we are going to progress. I have heard people say that they ignored red flags in relationships and even in business practices. Doing this negatively impacted their progress. Ignoring important facts that could delay or derail you is not a wise practice, especially if you are trying to save someone's feelings.

■ ■ ■

There is nothing worse than needing something and not being able to locate it. I reflect on the times when I needed to know what to do and this knowledge was not in plain sight. Have you ever been ready to walk out the door and suddenly realized that you cannot locate your keys? Frantically, you may have begun to search, maybe even tearing up the house as you looked for the vital item you needed. The point I am making is that the things we need are to be kept close that we may readily access them at the appreciate time. Direction, understanding, and wisdom are such things.

A direction is a course that something moves toward. A direction is also the WAY. Knowing the way is half the battle. You cannot start out on a journey without considering the path you should take. You will not make progress if you don't start. Years ago, I got a revelation that transition is not a location but a passageway. It is not a destination but a bypass route. We often refer to bypasses as detours. A detour is a notification that you are not on the main route and that you have not arrived at your destination, but when you are on a bypass, you can recognize that if you stay the course, you will arrive at the intended address.

4

CHAOS

I am a naturally orderly person. A lack of order causes dysfunction for me, but for each person, this experience is different. Personally, I become outraged when I am in the midst of things that are out of order. This doesn't mean that I am the most organized person by nature; however, it does mean that I recognize that structure aids in my peace and healthy functioning. Having order is my safe haven.

■ ■ ■

Recently, I have examined this idea, as I have been searching for contentment. Sometimes we don't need money, but we need contentment and order. Even if you have lots of money and no order, you still have chaos and unhappiness. Chopping tomatoes and cucumbers is a tedious task that I can't say is my favorite, but it causes me less stress to eat something healthy. Therefore, I acknowledge that taking thirty minutes to wash and chop fruits and vegetables makes my life happier. My stomach is getting flatter, and I can see my efforts paying off. This is what makes me happy—it is not the process itself, per se. It's called order. I don't like it, but I need it. Having order is a necessity for me.

■ ■ ■

Management is not overseeing people. It is a fashion in which processes and substances are stewarded. It is measuring/tracking and delegating of work, resources, time, and energy. A manager is someone who collaborates with a team to get a goal accomplished. She/he is a strategist. My primary goal is to live well and use methods to accomplish my goals. Living well does not take a lot of money; it takes mindfulness. At work, I was asked what foods I do or don't like. I responded: "I eat to live now rather than living to eat." As you can see, my response was not a simple list of foods, but a reflection of my mindset to live well through my diet. So, I can say that I don't eat something or don't like something because it speaks against living well. Indulg-

> *"You have to be intentional in your efforts as you exhibit characteristics of pursuing your dreams."*

ing in food that makes me fat and or will harm me does not equate to living well. Therefore, I love what makes me well in spite of the taste or preparation required to eat it.

DISTRACTIONS

Attention deficit disorder is a legitimate reason to wrestle with distractions. Those with this challenge are heroes because they endeavor to excel despite their challenges with focusing. With that being said, there is a legitimate reason that people struggle with focusing. While this is the issue for some, the majority of us are not struggling with focus due to having ADHD. We might not always be aware of the things that distract us; one example of this is unconscious behavior that we might engage in when something catches us off guard. For instance, we might give time to unexpected phone calls or a visit from a neighbor.

However, some distractions can be very deliberate ones that we engage in to avoid an activity or to put off a task you do not enjoy. Wait a minute—this is not the part where you get hammered for being lazy or judged as such. This is the part where we discover—or even uncover—that we often welcome distractions more than we will openly admit.

Being occupied with unimportant things and people are distractions. At times, however, we may actually *need* distractions. Let me explain. Being preoccupied to the degree of worry is counterproductive and does not add to your progress. A productive activity can distract us taking our focus away from worrying. If you are going to progress in life, you must guard your focus. I will discuss focus later in the book. Here we must recognize the distractions that can unnecessarily make our lives chaotic.

Dividing your focus between five or six things is possible it's called multitasking. The brain is designed to have multiple activities happening in the body at once, this is natural a process but you have to discipline your coordination to think, speak and act. For instance, dancing and singing comes natural to some performers, others need to focus more intentionally on dancing than signing because their coordination to dance and sing simultaneously is challenging. With that being said, if you know multitasking is not your strength devote your time to the areas where you can be productive choosing quality of focus over quantity of deeds.

Consequently, distractions are often used as excuses for being unproductive. I heard a preacher on a social media broadcast say something worthy of sharing with you: "Making an excuse for where you are is building a case to stay where you are." Justifying excuses is a defense for the distractions that make your life chaotic, hectic and unproductive. To progress I encourage you to conclude no distraction is worth your productivity or your time focus.

BACKGROUND NOISE

You'd be surprised how many people I meet who refuse to go out to dinner alone. I also know people—men and women—who will not cook a meal at home because they enjoy preparing food for a person or eating a meal with a person more than doing it alone. Being the only one at the table may feel awkward, but eating alone can provide you with an opportunity to be with your thoughts, as we have no other distractions and can give our much-deserved thoughts some time to be recognized.

■ ■ ■

There are many reasons to appreciate quietness.

Meditating on good thoughts and words, future successes, or even the goodness you have already experienced are good reasons to appreciate quietness. If you are on the go, meaning you live a busy lifestyle as most people do, caring for their families and working, then you will likely have to create opportunities for quietness. is less about noise and more about disturbance. When a test is being given usually there is a sign posted on door or noticeably displayed. The sign cautions others not to behave in a disturbing manner. In public libraries the atmosphere is quite not silent there is a difference. Silence is no noise at all and quietness could include soft noise. Like, speaking in a whisper and moving not to be a disturbance to others who maybe studying or reading. Quite time can be used for focus and concentration or reflection. **Here's a key:** <u>Having intentional focus and reflection time, will help us allow our attention to impact where it's needed.</u> We may discover how to rid our life of stress, figure out a problem, relax, and get revived. All through our having intentional calm moments.

■ ■ ■

When people are avoiding things, they may turn on the television or play music when they arrive home. It is not that they are truly listening but that they would rather fill the atmosphere with noise that doesn't make it so obvious that they are alone. Background noise then becomes company. Having company is not a bad thing; in fact, fellowship is good, needed even. However, company is not good when it is a distraction. We tell our teens that their friends can't come over because they have homework or chores to do. It's likely that the teens will be sipping tea, spilling tea (this is a hip term for gossiping), texting, or prowling social media. The mature-aged crowd is familiar with the idea of "not taking company." The older folks—our parents—felt that if we had company when we were supposed to be focusing on accomplishing a task, we might never achieve our goals.

5

BED OF EASE

You may be wondering, how can comfort be my enemy? In this chapter, I refer to being comfortable as lying in a bed of ease. To begin, nothing great you achieve will be done on a flowery bed of ease. There will be opposition when you decide to progress. This is not a sermonette telling you that you need to adapt to a hard life; instead, this is a tool to help you discover the comforts in your life that are serving as roadblocks to your progress.

"Those who were rebuilding the wall and those who carried burdens took their load with one hand doing the work and the other holding a weapon," Nehemiah 4:17 (KJV). Miraculously, this group of workers committed

to help Nehemiah, I characterize as builders (intentional and focused minded people), shared the burden of rebuilding the wall they worked nonstop to complete. The mission was to rebuild the wall; it was not a time to be social or relaxed. Let me ask you a question: are you in a relaxed position right now when you should work on your assignment to help you progress in life? The Message translation of Ecclesiastes 3:1 says, *"there's an opportune time to do things, a right time for everything on the earth."* In my words, allow me to say the same thing: there is a time for comfort and a time for discomfort. In a state of comfort, a man and woman may date, get married, and then decide to have children. Perhaps for years they enjoyed the comfort and freedom of each other, but for nine months, there will be the discomfort of carrying a child (and much more discomfort is coming when it's time for the woman to give birth). The process of progress in having a child is far from easy.

■ ■ ■

Life, my friends, is not entirely about peace and comfort. That same passage of Ecclesiastes tells us that there will be a time of war and a time of peace. Allow this entry to speak to your heart about the habits and comforts that are working against you as you aim to progress in your life. I love the results of working out; however, I do not take pleasure in experiencing sore muscles or in pushing myself to be disciplined when perhaps I am already exhausted. I could not meet my fitness and health goals by reclining seven days a week in comfort. I take a day reprieve every three to four days to give my body a rest. To progress in this area, I cannot eat what I want—comfort foods filled with fats, sugars, and carbs—three to four days a week and expect to be the same weight or have a healthy body. This fact is relatable to the lesson taught in 1 Timothy 4:8. Which teaches that discipline is needed in both the physical and spiritual aspects of our life. Isolating this concept to physical exercise of the body will do little for your overall progress.

KEYS THAT PROMOTE PROGRESS

1. You can progress by connecting to someone more successful than you in the area you desire to expand, someone else's knowledge and experience can benefit you causing you to grow and evolve to where God is taking you.

2. Take a stand say what God says about you often so that you will cultivate a positive internal voice.

3. Apply intentional effort where you need and desire progress.

4. Having intentional focus and reflection time will help us allow our attention to impact where it's needed.

5. If you are going to progress in life, you must see yourself the way God sees you.

6. The source to having courage is to find what motivates you.

7. Make it harder for yourself to quit by making it easier to succeed.

8. Having the confidence to cope with life as it happens will empower you.

9. Having self-confidence—with or without money—will make you that much more attractive to others.

10. If you are going to progress, knowing the habits of your nature is important.

11. A weapon against the enemy of your progress is a confident heart!

PART 2

PRINCIPLES OF PROGRESS

6
EFFORT

You will get things accomplished when your focus is to act.

DEMONSTRATE CHARACTER

What you do each day is a demonstration of your character. "*Whom he called together with the workmen of like occupation, and said, Sirs, ye know that by this craft we have our wealth,*" Acts 19:25 (KJV). To progress in life, you must understand and implement the principles of progress. Your character fuels your attitude. I have a saying I repeat to myself: "I'm not saying you're a loser. I'm just saying I'm a champion!" The focus is not on competing; it's on demonstrating your winning character and behavior. Champions never show up to just compete; we show up to demonstrate.

Moreover, effort requires earnestness, zeal, and haste. Haste can be described as urgent movement. When Mary received news from the angel she would be having a baby she was filled with anticipation. *"And Mary arose in those days, and went into the hill country with haste, into a city of Juda,"* Luke 1:39 (KJV). I believe the reason Mary made haste making her way into the city of Juda was her anticipation to both see the demonstration of courage in her elder cousin Elizbeth who was also pregnant and be the demonstration of courage as a virgin but birthing a miracle.

■ ■ ■

Your character includes your strengths and weaknesses. How you do what you do is important. *"Or he that exhorteth, on exhortation: he that giveth, let him do it with simplicity; he that ruleth, with diligence; he that sheweth mercy, with cheerfulness,"* Rom. 12:8 (KJV).

■ ■ ■

Time is a record keeper of what you really want. You and your vision are one. You must eliminate the shadows, division, and unbelief that disconnect you from what you are born to produce. Your dream is within your DNA, and your perception of yourself can push you to accomplish your dreams or separate you from your dreams. A dream is an internal journey. You don't need anyone's approval to pursue your dreams. When you give birth to a child, he or she has your DNA, and through your DNA, you influence the characteristics and traits of your child. In the same manner, you influence the dream that lives within you. Turn your energy inwardly toward what is growing and developing on the inside of you. It is your dream—just as your child is yours—created and established from your own blood. Champions have characteristics that allow them to build something that comes from within.

■ ■ ■

How do you demonstrate that you are a dreamer? In order for me to say that you are funny, I would need to observe something about you that you have expressed that indicates that you are humorous. Comedians do this is intentionally and deliberately. Their goal is to make you laugh. You have to be intentional in your efforts as you exhibit characteristics of pursuing your dreams. For instance, determination, drive, initiative and commitment are visible in the life of a person excitedly pursing their dreams.

The ant has the characteristics of a hard worker. It has the characteristics to save. It will save, relentlessly work, strive, and passionately pursue its daily mission to conserve food for the winter. It takes hard work to build a kingdom. The ant has to lift food twice its size as it realizes that its survival and the survival of its family depend on its ability to produce. I wonder how your life might change if you were to wake up every day with these characteristics. To this point, I will share with you some things I did with effort and consistency in my life.

■ ■ ■

What I had to realize was that I needed to have a deliberate attitude in accomplishing the smallest task or achieve my professional and personal goals. In other words, I planned, I thought, I pursued them, I wrote action lists, I set reminders on my mobile calendar, I established accountability with people and technology. Yes, technology. Most mobile applications we use have alerts or notifications that can be set to remind you to perform a task or an action step to help us meet our goals. If you are serious about meeting your goals accountability can help you progress in meeting your goals. I see accountability as it an effort meter measuring deliberate actions.

■ ■ ■

Effort comes with your undivided attention. Be aware that your attention is usually stolen by an unplanned event or thought that leads to action. Execute the immediate and plan well so that you can keep your focus on your priorities. If you are doing your homework and the phone suddenly rings, your immediate thought may be to make sure there are no emergencies. Afterward, you might plan to address the purpose for the interruption as a second priority.

■ ■ ■

You will not make effort toward a goal that is not interesting to you. Value your interests enough to protect your interests. There is a simple but powerful quote I love by Bishop T.D. Jakes: "Your interests make you interesting." These are the things that delight you and bring you enjoyment, the things that pique your interest and makes you curious enough to pursue them. Attentiveness is a channel of energy; when the channel closes, your attention is gone. Then it's impossible to get back the energy or flow you had before the disruption took place. You will grasp for it; you may even come close to getting it back. Rarely, though, will you totally capture that uniqueness of thought again—unless, that is, you are able to access the portal of attention a second time. Someone once said, "God is not obligated to speak twice." The premise here is that it is important that you don't take your attention for granted.

7
EXECUTION

Mark Twain said, "There are a thousand excuses for failure but never a good reason."

The definition of execution is to carry out a plan, order, or course of action. <u>You must follow through on a thought or plan with the purpose to accomplish something.</u> What are you really thinking about? To achieve the things you desire, you must begin with thinking intentionally. What you do after a good thought is important. When you have a good idea, do you write it down, or do you allow it to escape? Do you respond or allow it to float away? Prioritize your actions. "The road to hell was paved with good intentions." John Ray (1860). This English proverb means it is not enough to simply mean to do well, one must act to do well.

■ ■ ■

A good friend of mine always says, "Hope is not a strategy." We must do something beyond hoping. Recently, I put on my inaugural women's event in Atlanta, Georgia. I now know the value of prioritizing because of this experience. Taking an audit of what is necessary—in the order of first, second, and third on the list of priorities—is a necessity. From this experience, I learned that I needed to be flexible in the event that my plans went awry. The women's event was a success, as I sold out of tickets, but I did not fully think through how to pay for services rendered from the band, the caterer and the event planner. Furthermore, I noticed some things that we executed poorly like guests that were paying at the door were waiting in line due to having only one person stationed for payments, there was an online registration for the conference as tickets sold I counted on having funds to pay caterer from the sells. Unfortunately, I did not understand I would not get full payment from ticket sells until a week after the event. This caused me to breach a few contracts where I agreed to pay before the event date. The aforementioned challenges put me at risk that possibly people would not want to come to any of my future events or business owners may refuse to do business with me based on the experience being spoken about from other people. Lastly, I did not have enough volunteers to help clean the venue I rented. Having more volunteers for clean-up would have allowed more to get done easier and much sooner.

Overall, things that we executed well and the positive turn out had a greater impact on me, personally, given this was my first event living in a new city. The merchant vendors were organized in their assigned stations, the sound system functioned with quality, the music and the DJ were festive and engaging with the crowd, the food menu was suitable and the food tasty. The award recipients were all present. Women came from various places it was a well-attended event.

This is exactly why I have determined that early planning is necessary. Execution, simply put, requires that you follow through. Ask yourself, have I chosen laziness over order? Having frequently chosen laziness myself, I know that laziness is overlooking a task. Yep! You just turn your head like you don't even see it. It is allowing things to be unkempt. You may not be aware of all that you need when you embark upon an endeavor. However, following through can lead to the next steps to what is needed to accomplish what you set out to do. Follow through is as easy as returning a phone call, responding to an email or text message. Follow-through helps you conclude a matter, it means working down your list of this to do that will bring the results of finishing. Follow-through is execution that leads to progress. You may be more effective finding a method to organize the actions that helps you stay focused in getting things done. I am a lists person. I can execute action steps and keep focus to complete tasks if there in list form. The result of finding a method of actions will possibly reduce inspire you.

■ ■ ■

As I mentioned before, one of the things that sends me over the edge in my personal life is needing something and not being able to put my hands on it. How frustrating it is to not be organized. I despise when I spend valuable time looking everywhere for a document because it was not where it should have been. I also cannot stand having to be somewhere and arriving late because I didn't map out where I was going, particularly when I am a presenter or a speaker. To avoid this, I make a to do list. Then at times I write down probing questions to help minimize my list. Here is an exercise that could help in you organize actions or probe your thinking to see what you discover. Ask yourself the questions below to determine the depth of your drive to execute.

1. Have you chosen to delay your future by ignoring your present priorities?
2. What level of importance have you ranked your relationships, your health, your money, and your dreams?
3. Where have you set the bar? Setting the bar means setting a standard.
4. What standard have you set to progress?
5. How does your life look on paper? In other words, are there action steps that will equal the outcome you want written in a journal or someplace where you can visibility measure your progress?

> *"To progress, you will need execution over excuses."*

You may think you manage your schedule well until you see how off task you are as you keep a time log. You will see how many tasks you actually execute and others that are past due for a follow-up. The same is true with a budget—without one, you will overspend, as you do not track where your dollars go. Likewise, with your dietary habits, unless you record the calories you have taken in and the ones you have burned, you will be completely unconscious of your progress or lack thereof.

■ ■ ■

Are you taking your time for granted? Putting off things you can do now is taking for granted the time that we have, as we believe that we will always have the time or opportunity later. It's my opinion that one of the biggest things we take for granted is time. Let's compare this with pregnancy. When you are pregnant, you will not be in the first or second trimester forever. When you are pregnant with something, there is a set time to bring it forward. It could be nine months, twelve months, or three years—there is a set time to push out what you carry. If you chronicled your life from 6 a.m. to 9 p.m., would you be on task throughout your day? In particular, apps can be helpful to help you track your time, as well as your finances, fitness, notes—pretty much anything. Use as many apps as possible to help you carry out the most important plans that will help you progress daily. We always take for granted the things that we neglect. When we neglect our goals, we create barriers to our progress. If it needs to be done, don't put much thought into it; just get it done. **Apply this principle:** _To progress, you will need execution over excuses._

8

INTENTIONAL SHIFTS

Labor requires intentional shifts. One of the greatest lessons I learned about labor came from a successful man I will call Wellington. He is a pastor and business man. He is on television three times a day. In addition to his television shows, he has written books and owns a barbershop. His church runs a youth program, and the congregation is a beacon of light in the community. I mention all of this to explain that he knows hard work. As I was talking to him one day, I was expressing that nothing I did was working and that I had done everything to change my situation. He responded very wisely. He said, "You may have done a few things, but you haven't done everything."

His words were piercing. I then began to examine my intentions. That conversation birthed a new concept in me—I realized it was important to work hard not only to get something done but also to cause a shift. What Wellington expressed to me allowed me to see I may have tried a few things but my level of intensity and consistency would cause me to see a difference in my life. For this reason, I needed to apply some specific efforts. Application means putting in work or action (google dictionary). Intensity can express the magnitude of force or strength that can cause your work to profit. Saying to my friend that nothing was working, what I meant was that my situation had not yet changed. Specifically, I was referring to my financial position that was affecting others areas in my life. Although I felt that I was making effect to change it is was not changing. What I later concluded was I had not created a momentum that would cause change in my life. Not that I was doing anything wrong when I made my complaint that nothing I was doing was working, I wasn't persevering in what I was doing for a reason, I wasn't following an effort long enough or with enough intensity to make an impact. Work creates momentum, and momentum causes a shift. Eventually, change in my financial position came. I got completely out of my comfort zone doing different things like becoming more conscious of my financial habits, upgraded my skillset in a position I absolutely did not want to be in and tirelessly applying for jobs I thought would open a career path for growth, longevity and increase in pay.

> *"In order to progress, you will have to labor to create a momentum of intentional shifts in your life that bring about good change."*

I adopted the same attitude about my weight and physical fitness. Now when I work out, my intention is to sweat. Whether I do low-impact or high-impact exercise, the result will be the same—burning calories. I know when I have reached a momentum when I run. During this time, my chest is open, my breathing has a steady rhythm, and there is a force pushing me to make strides. All of these signs let me know I am going somewhere. Even if I feel uncomfortable I keep picking up my legs motioning to go forward I have come to value the discomfort of momentum.

■ ■ ■

Putting in the work will make you sweat. If you ain't sweating, you ain't working! I attended a one-day fitness boot camp the fitness trainer said to the class, "You are not performing because you are thinking about the pain you feel presently." Your focus has to be on the work, not the pain. As I looked around at the other participants in the class their physical disposition it was visible that they were definitely uncomfortable. To make it through the class I closed my eyes giving it all I had focusing on finishing and not how hard it was to perform each exercise. The bottom line is I had to get committed to habits that bring about change, not to quit, or complain because I was uncomfortable. Bishop Gary Hall, Sr. pastor of the West Jacksonville Church of God in Christ in Jacksonville, Florida says, "bad habits will fight you back." You can say to herself you are going to change but your habits will fight you back. As he preached his sermon he described how bad habits won't change easily. Changing bad social affiliations, eating patterns and financial habits when they have been a part of your life will not come without work. Apply this principle: <u>In order to progress, you will have to labor to create a momentum of intentional shifts in your life that bring about good change.</u>

9
PROGRESS OF EXISTENCE

Oxford Dictionary definition of Time is "the indefinite continued progress of existence and events in the past, present, and future regarded as a whole." What are you really doing with your time? I believe that people waste time because they are terrified of facing what is or could be boredom. Boredom by my definition, is the inability to be interested in exploring the self or the lack of interest in discovering new things. Therefore, we allow people to be what we pursue, and our inordinate interest in others leads us to lose in ourselves. This alone is a waste of time my friends. The time we spend lost and disconnected from ourselves and our purpose can lead to life ending prematurely. Simply because there was a disconnect of purpose and time.

At length, certain events in my life propelled me to transform pain and grief into victory. I can trace that transformation back to a place in time. In particular, picking up the pieces of my education by going back to school to get my high school diploma. I preceded into college to pursue a communications degree. Developing the discipline to study was no drop in the bucket. In fact, I had to be careful not to compare my learning capacity with others because it looked so easy for them; while for me, there were times I found myself struggling with my classes. I had to tell myself often that God knew the obstacles outside of my control. I had to stay consistent to pursue my academic goals, and to this day I am intentional in what I learn. My constant intent is to "study to show myself approved unto God," 2 Timothy 2:15 (KJV). Which means I do not look to other people to determine how smart I am. My approval comes from God and the graceful ability to accomplish what He has given me to accomplish. I allowed my studying to be a time growth.

■ ■ ■

Earlier, I shared when I was attacked. Over time I realized my tendency to stuff my emotions away and not properly process nor mourn my experience. This means I did not express my anger, frustration, and distress from this experience. However, anger would surface over the smallest situations or I would explode with emotional outbursts in times of pressure. I would overreact and collapse into tears feeling powerless and overwhelmed. Going to counseling helped me work through the intense emotions that would surface in my life. I went to counseling for two years. When I started counseling, I did not have a time frame of how long I would go. I made an intentional decision that my fragile life was worth one hour a week. After a couple of months, the appointment times expanded further and further apart. I went until I saw significant progress and was confident that I was better. I was able to manage my emotions, my overall esteem improved, my thoughts about my family and separation we went through changed. I realized it was not my fault. I addressed issues that impacted my life as a whole. Over time I began to heal. I had a sense of what being happy was and how to move on with my life. If you are going to progress you must seriously evaluate what's holding you back address it then use your time in continuous connection with interest and purpose.

> *"Confidence to do something comes from knowing God has given you the potential to get it done; your part is to develop and pursue the desired goal."*

■ ■ ■

My life is the epitome of intentions to make efforts to produce something great. Life can give you every reason to make excuses why you should not do something or why you should quit at the first sign of inconvenience or adversity. I wrote this book for people who struggle with bringing forth greatness and dreams. Naturally, with all the insecurities I had I wasted a lot of time procrastinating and feeling like I was not good enough. As result, I didn't get much accomplished behaving this way. **Apply this principle:** <u>Confidence to do something comes from knowing God has given you the potential to get it done; your part is to develop and pursue the desired goal.</u>

10
PURSUING PROGRESS

When I started my journey to accomplish things in life, I quickly concluded that I lacked support. I was a new believer, and I felt alone. I believed that the people around me did not understand and that they could not connect with where I desired to go. My goal at this time was to grow as a Christian. I had an unquenchable thirst and would stop at nothing to grow. I attended multiple church services a week. I went to revivals and outreach meetings, and I got involved in the church by volunteering my time to help with things that interested me.

My goal was to be full of the word of God, so I prayed and studied all the time. I was so engaged in my interest that I shared it with my mother, brother, and sister. At that time, they showed little to no interest in the things that I was showing so much interest in. So, yes, I found myself alone. When I started preaching, I'd invite them, but they would not come. When I began to share my joy that I felt because I was a Christian, it was also not a topic of interest. I learned that if I wanted to stay encouraged, I would need to walk alone.

■ ■ ■

When we develop our interests, we progress in our lives, and we increase our joy and peace. I did not attend high school, which is a time in which most people find a sport they enjoy or socialize with friends. However, I have developed my interests along the way. This took time, and it required me to invest in myself to discover who I am and what makes me happy. When you invest yourself, you set yourself up to reap later joy. I believe this process is a bridge to self-confidence.

■ ■ ■

The pursuit of progress may end up being a lonely walk. I have preached in many places. Ninety-five percent of the time, I was alone. The people I most wanted to be there showed no interest in being there.

When I started making Christian friends, it was because I attended church functions, and the people there began to encourage me to become involved and get to know new people. My support system began to include people who were already on the same journey I was, and I realized that they could shed light and help in my growth and development. I can remember looking into a crowd of people from the pulpit, thinking that I didn't know anyone there and that there were no familiar faces in the crowd. As most speakers get to the podium, they would acknowledge the family members who were attending with them. I was not able to do that because I was alone. I can remember feeling ready to burst into tears before preaching one time, and the Holy Spirit spoke assuredly in my ear, "You are not alone." Even as I write this, tears well up inside me because it is so true. As God told Joshua, *"No one will be able to stand against you all the days of your life As I was with Moses, so will I be with you; I will never leave you nor forsake you," Joshua 1:5 (KJV).*

I mention earlier, the pursuit of success and progress can be a lonely walk. I don't look back much anymore, but over the years, I have come to understand why my early days were so lonely. When we want to be accepted by others, they can really influence our decisions, including our likes and dislikes. In my early years, I asked God why I was so isolated. Actually, the conversation went like this: "God, when will you let people be in my life?" He responded, *"When you don't need them."* I came to understand that this answer was the saving grace that gave me fire in my pursuit of doing better. I became dependent only on God and sought my acceptance only from Him, as well. This shift eliminated my insecurities. Obeying what God called me to do has been the greatest affirmation I could ever have. Natural support from the people in our lives is instrumental, but when it is not available, we must go to the Father. See your isolated times and seasons as protection, not alienation.

■ ■ ■

MOTIVES IN PURSUING

A strong pursuit is needed for you to go after what you desire. I desired a change in my lineage and in my immediate family. I was the youngest of three, and neither my brother nor my sister received their high school diploma. I hated the way that other people saw us when I was younger. My mother was a single parent struggling with lifelong alcoholism. Statistically, we were doomed to repeat the same types of behavior. But my motivation to be better drove me to pursue change.

■ ■ ■

Dropping out of school in the eighth grade to take care of myself was a big setback in my education. Lying on job applications about my age and level of education came to an end once employers began asking me for copies of my records. I had to change. I pursued education first, starting with getting a GED. Because I earned my GED, I have forever changed the narrative of my immediate family; before I earned it, the narrative was that none of my mother's children had a high school diploma. It was difficult to learn to read past the eighth-grade level because I had walked away from formal learning. I was fourteen years old when I left school, and I earned my GED at the age of twenty-five. My motive was to close an eleven-year gap of ignorance in my life and even more importantly to close the gap in my lineage. Accomplishing this was the hardest thing I have ever done in my life.

PURSUIT OF CHANGE AS A MOTIVE

Pursuing change is uncomfortable. However, it is through that pursuit that I find my motive for progress. There I was, the youngest of three children, and I had to be the one to change and set an example by becoming formally educated. My pursuit of change is both a motive and an example for my daughter and my siblings' children. Progress for my family is demonstrated through discipline and hard work. **A key** to progress is the understanding that most of the problems we have are not people problems; they are character problems. The pursuit of progress has multiple challenges but the difficulty is not about the situation; it's about our character. Through hard work and discipline the impact of change is beyond our situation but extends to our character as a person. This process then serves as a motivation for progress.

PROGRESSING AT ANY COST

Because I was in pursuit of God, I did whatever was required. I spent hours reading my Bible to get an understanding of the life He gave to me. Most Christians want to come to church to receive a message, but they never actually experience the glory of God.

■ ■ ■

In most situations, thirst drives your pursuit and progress. As I have shared, I was kidnapped and raped at gunpoint. However, I had a choice to make: I could choose to be fearful and never go out at night again, or I could choose to live a life of freedom. After this incident, I was afraid even to close the shower curtain when I bathed. When I would walk, I would look over my shoulder every few seconds. I was a nervous wreck until I realized that I had become a victim of fear. My thirst to be free from the bondage that fear had placed me it drove me to change. I began to put the word of God to work to help me get my life back. It has been said so many times: change comes when you want it badly enough. How badly do you want it?

■ ■ ■

> *"Find a way to invest in yourself to develop peace and joy in your life."*

The details that I have written here are recollections of true events. While I did not include my entire life story, I have given you the principles that really moved my life forward. When I was in a dilemma or just wondering how to get beyond the position I wanted to change, I would follow these principles. I invite you to reread this book to get a precise understanding of how you want to progress. Follow the principles, and make it happen. **Apply this principle:** <u>Find a way to invest in yourself to develop peace and joy in your life.</u>

<u>PRINCIPLES OF PROGRESS</u>

1. Find a way to invest in yourself to develop peace and joy in your life.
2. Confidence to do something comes from knowing God has given you the potential to get it done; your part is to develop and pursue the desired goal.
3. In order to progress, you will have to labor to create a momentum of intentional shifts in your life that bring about good change.
4. To progress, you will need execution over excuses.
5. Take a stand say what God says about you often so that you will cultivate a positive internal voice.

ABOUT THE AUTHOR

Natasha Davis is an inspiring young woman. She has lived a life of commitment and dedication to her, faith, and community. As an ordained minister, Natasha has been blessed to travel the world in pursuit of nurturing and growing the Kingdom of God. It is through her faith-walk, world travels, and her prayer and meditation that she shares her thoughts and insights with her readers. Prepare to accompany her as she shares the moments of learning and insight she has experienced throughout her life. Natasha's unique storytelling and her insightful reflection combine to carry the reader through a wonderful journey of life and discovery.

Natasha currently lives in the Greater Atlanta Metropolitan area with her daughter. She is actively engaged in parenting, ministry and community engagement. She has already begun to put together her thoughts and ideas for her next project. Natasha is eternally grateful for your support and partnership on her initial launch into the world of publishing. She is excited to have you along and looks forward to continuing this journey together in the coming years.

9 781513 661131